The LieOGraphy

of

THOMAS EDISON

The Absolutely Untrue, Totally Made Up,
100% Fake Life Story
of the World's Greatest Inventor

by Alan Katz
illustrations by TRACY HILL

Tanglewood • Indianapolis

Published by Tanglewood Publishing, Inc.
Text © 2020 Alan Katz
Illustrations © 2020 Tracy Hill

Cover and Interior art by Tracy Hill
Design by Amy Alick Perich

Tanglewood Publishing, Inc.
1060 N. Capitol Ave., Ste. E-395
Indianapolis, IN 46204
www.tanglewoodbooks.com

Printed in the USA by Gasch Printing, LLC.
10 9 8 7 6 5 4 3 2

ISBN 978-1-939100-47-4

Library of Congress Control Number: 2020940192

Dedication:

To Natalie and Sol,
who invented _me_

One

If Thomas Edison were alive today, he'd be well over 160 years old. And while the man is credited with more than 1,000 life-changing inventions, a machine to allow him to live 160+ years was not one of them. So sadly, he is not here today to tell his fascinating story.

The good news, however, is that Mr. Edison lives on through his scientific achievements, as well as through the words in his top secret diary, which has never been found and indeed may not even exist.

You are about to read the tale of a man who looked at what was, thought about what is, and invented what could be. A man who never accepted the word "no," never stopped dreaming, never stopped thinking, never stopped trying, and never drank a cup of fruit punch with a scrambled egg in it.

It's the tale of a man who never stopped asking why, never stopped asking how, never stopped asking when, never stopped asking who, and never realized that the capital letter M looks quite a lot like an upside down capital letter W.

And it's the tale of a man who, in many ways, made it possible for you to communicate with others, watch movies, read books, and get long, difficult, impossible to complete homework assignments.

It's time to meet Thomas Irving Edison.

Two

Thomas Irving Edison was invented, well, born, on the 407th day of 1846. Many considered the day to be part of February 1847, but Thomas' parents were great believers in getting the most out of a year, so they very often ignored New Year's Eve and just kept counting days well past the 365 that most people say make up a year.

See, they too were quite inventive.

Thomas came from a large family; he was the eighth of seven kids, and often wore hand-me-down clothes and ate hand-me-down food. As a young child, he pretty much lived on sandwiches the family called

TABAPI, which stood for Take A Bite And Pass It.

As you might imagine, by the time a tuna on white bread got to little Thomas, all he had was crust. Maybe that's why he ate tuna at pretty much every meal as an adult—even at breakfast. And maybe it's also the reason he got extremely angry whenever anyone said the words TABAPI (which hardly ever happened) or crust (which he heard quite often). Those who considered Thomas Edison an ill-tempered man were those who said those words to him; to everyone else, he was a kind, friendly, sweet man of invention.

As a boy, Thomas—or Tomolino, as he was called in a language no one in his family understood—considered himself an inventor from the time he could first say the words, "I consider myself an inventor." And when people would ask, "What's an inventor?" the young man would reply, "It's something I invented. And it's what I am."

No one really understood. But they knew Tomolino was headed for big fame...or big trouble. And they couldn't wait to find out which it would be.

From age five on, Tomolino loved to play with trains. Unfortunately, they were real trains, with real locomotive engines. The boy would sit high upon a hill, always keeping a safe distance from the tracks, and he'd use a homemade "remote control" device to make the trains run.

The device was quite simple: three dirty sticks tied together. It did absolutely nothing other than swing back and forth.

But Tomolino would sit on the hill at precisely 2:27 p.m. each day and wave the device up and down until the train came. When it was nearing the station, Tomolino would wave the device back and forth to

make it slow down and stop. He'd pull on the left stick and people would get off. Then he'd pull on the right stick and the doors would close and the train would start moving. And he'd pull on the center stick to make the train speed up...until it was out of sight.

No one had the heart to tell Tomolino that his device had nothing to do with the train's arrival or departure. He believed in it his whole life. In fact, he'd get mad whenever he'd see a train motoring down the tracks, figuring that someone had ripped off his idea and was using a similar "three sticks tied together" device to run the trains.

So seeing a train, or hearing the words TABAPI or crust made Edison mad; most other times, he was a kind, friendly, sweet man of invention.

Three

Besides the train device—which we now know was pretty much nothing—most consider Edison's first invention to be the Reading Machine.

Despite its name, the Reading Machine was not actually a machine. It was simply just another stick, which he used to poke his big brother Elliot in the ribs until he agreed to read to him.

Elliot would be doing his homework, or sitting quietly, and Tomolino would jab him with the Reading Machine and Elliot would sigh and start reading aloud to Tomolino. The more Tomolino jabbed, the more Elliot

read. It would go on like that for hours a day, ending only when Elliot lost his voice... or when it was time for Tomolino to make the 2:27 train arrive.

(After awhile, Tomolino even invented something to prevent Elliot from losing his voice; he patented it as an invention he called The Glass of Water.)

On his sixth birthday, Tomolino changed his name back to Thomas, and from that day on, got extremely angry with anyone that called him Tomolino.

So hearing the words TABAPI or crust, seeing a train, or being called Tomolino made Edison mad; most other times, he was a kind, friendly, sweet man of invention.

In school, the young lad quickly became known as a kid with different ideas, someone who tried to take learning far beyond learning by questioning the obvious.

For example, one time when his teacher said, "One plus one equals two," Thomas raised his hand and asked, "Why?"

The teacher answered, "Because if you have one apple and you get another apple, you have two apples."

Thomas accepted that, and then raised his hand to ask, "What about plums?"

The teacher said, "Yes, plums too. One plum plus one plum equals two plums."

"Grapes?"

"Yes."

"Zebras?"

"Yes."

"Piano stools?"

"Yes."

"Coyotes?"

"Yes."

"Gobs of earwax?"

"Yes."

"Socks?

"Yes."

"Buckets of sand?"

"Yes! One of something plus one of something always equals two of that thing!"

"Even puppies?"

"Yes."

"Guppies?"

"Yes."

"Wuppies?"

"Yes."

"I have a question..."

"Yes?"

"What are wuppies?"

At that point, the teacher sent Thomas to

the principal's office. And when the principal called in the assistant principal, Thomas counted; he was in trouble with one person and then with another person—which meant he was indeed in trouble with *two* people.

His teacher had been right!

Four

Now you might be thinking that Thomas Edison was a bit of a pain in the neck in school. But that really wasn't the case. Yes, he asked a lot of questions. Yes, he took apart many things that were working just fine. Yes, he yelled, "I have an idea!" even when he didn't have one, confident that he could probably come up with one by the time someone asked him what it was.

But rather than being considered a pain in the neck, Thomas was thought of as a genius. The phrase, "I don't know—let's ask Thomas" pretty much took over the school.

"How do we stop the door from squeaking?

"I don't know—let's ask Thomas."

"How do we keep the clock from running 12 hours fast?"

"I don't know—let's ask Thomas."

"How do we construct a new school library entirely out of saltines?"

"I don't know—let's ask Thomas."

"Why is Thomas doing laps in an empty swimming pool while wearing a tuxedo?"

"I don't know—let's ask Thomas."

Ask Thomas they did. And more often than not, Thomas was able to figure out an immediate—and brilliant—answer.

Thomas won the school Science Fair so many times that the other kids started calling it the Science Unfair.

One year, while classmates John Harper and Glenn Meehan made a six-foot long spinning wheel water thing in a colorful bottle that proved without a doubt that water is wet, Thomas invented a brand new means of communication by tapping out signals. Here's what happened:

Thomas was sitting in a restaurant sipping milk, which for some reason he called Scode. After emptying his glass, he was still thirsty—so he tapped on the table and said, "Scode! Scode! More right now—please!"

He tapped hard. He tapped soft. He tapped long. He tapped short. And he found that when he tapped in a certain pattern, the waitress came much sooner. It was as if the taps were sending out a message!

This, dear reader, is how Edison came to invent More Scode, which was later renamed Morse Code and used by armies, navies, and others who needed to transmit information.

What became of Edison's classmates John Harper and Glenn Meehan? Did they end up as great scientists? Did they do amazing things for mankind? Did they succeed beyond their wildest dreams?

Why would you be thinking about *that*? This is, after all, *The Lieography of Thomas Irving Edison*.

Let's move on...

Five

How does an inventor get an idea? That's like asking how a matador gets a bull. Well, it's not exactly the same, but both inventor and matador end with "or," and both idea and bull have four letters, so that's *pretty close*.

For Thomas Edison, inventing was not a job; it was a way of life. Every day at precisely 11:01 am, 2:03 pm, 4:47 pm or 5:12 pm, he'd go into what he called ASTONISH MODE—which, amazingly, used the exact same letters in the words THOMAS EDISON. Really. Truly. Check it out for yourself. I'll wait.

When Thomas was struck with an idea, he'd often lock himself away and work on it and work on it until it was finished. Sometimes seconds turned into minutes turned into hours turned into days turned into weeks turned into months turned into years turned into decades turned into centuries before anyone would see him. But when the door would finally open and the inventor would emerge, he always had with him something no one had ever seen before.

His inventions saved time.

His inventions saved money.

His inventions saved lives.

But here's something interesting: while

Thomas Edison was a whiz at inventing important objects, he was *horrible* at keeping track of them. He'd invent something, then put it on the shelf. Several weeks later, he'd get the brilliant idea to invent the very same thing, work on it for months, and then go to put it on the shelf—only to realize he'd already invented that item.

This happened to Edison so many times that he finally sat down and figured out a way to never again put two identical inventions on the same shelf.

He went out and bought a whole bunch of extra shelves.

Six

It's said that 63%* of Americans are allergic to some type of food or plant.

For example, many people get runny noses or watery eyes if they eat fruit. For others, it's fish, nuts, or cheese that causes a reaction. And still others are allergic to roses, carnations, petunias, tulips, and violets.

Edison, however, did not have any allergies. In fact, there is no recorded evidence that the man sneezed even a single time in his entire life. Remarkable? Certainly. But if you made a list of remarkable things about Thomas Edison, it would be the

*Could be more, could be less. Could be much more, could be much less.

length of both of your outstretched arms, plus someone else's outstretched arm, which is not only quite long, but also very hard to figure out, since hardly anyone will lend you an outstretched arm these days.

By and large, Edison was a healthy man. Perhaps this was due to the two-mile walk he took every morning of his adult life. No matter the outside temperature, he'd get up at 6 a.m. and walk one mile, then have his friend Bernie drive him back home via horse and buggy. A minute later, Edison would walk another mile, and then Bernie would again drive him home.

Someone once asked Mr. Edison why he didn't just walk home after his first mile, thereby completing a two-mile walk without having to bother Bernie.

"Two important reasons," the inventor replied. "One, I don't know the way. And two, I enjoy bothering Bernie."

How did Bernie feel about having to do all that horse and buggy driving? Well, he really didn't mind, because the very generous Mr. Edison gave Bernie the worldwide rights to his invention of the invisible sewing machine. Bernie had orders for more than 10,000 invisible sewing machines (at $200 each!), but unfortunately misplaced the original and never saw it again.

Yet while he didn't make a fortune on the invention Edison had given him, Bernie did make quite a bit of money by conducting "Come Watch Thomas Edison Sleep" tours. Bernie charged $1 per person for these during-the-night tours (kids ages 4, 6 and 7 were free). For their dollar, visitors got to tiptoe into Edison's bedroom and watch the inventor snooze and snore. For an extra 25¢, they got to use his toothbrush on the way out of his house. For many, this would be the only brush with greatness they'd ever have.

Seven

"Thomas, come here, I need you," his mother called from the kitchen one bright summer morning in November 1869. Thomas, who was visiting his parents for the weekend, came running into the kitchen with a wrench, a pair of pliers, two feet of copper wire, and some pancake syrup.

"What is it, dear sweet mother?" Thomas asked as he breathlessly ran to her.

"Thomas, you're known throughout the world as well as in New Jersey as a man who invents something every day," she said.

"Right," he replied.

"Well my son, my son, I am in need of an invention," she told him.

"Right," he replied, always glad to help.

"See these pancakes?" she asked, pointing to a plate of delicious-looking pancakes.

"Right," he replied.

"Well, I made too many," she informed him.

"Right," he replied, suddenly glad he'd brought along pancake syrup.

"So, I would like you to invent a flying machine so that I could soar high above the clouds and bring the extra pancakes to my Cousin Fran in Texas."

"Wright, Wright," he replied.

"I said, I would like you to invent a flying machine so that I could soar high above the clouds and bring the extra pancakes to my Cousin Fran in Texas."

"Wright, Wright," he replied.

"Enough saying, 'right, right'; why aren't you inventing already?"

"I'm not saying 'right, right,'" he answered. "I'm saying 'Wright, Wright.' Listen closely to the silent 'W'."

"You want me to listen to silence? Maybe you've been working too hard. Maybe you should invent a good, long nap."

"Wright, Wright," he said.

"When will you stop this foolishness?" his mother pleaded.

Thomas stopped. "Dear sweet mother," he said. "I am not saying 'right, right' because I am agreeing with you. I am saying 'Wright, Wright' because two brothers I know named Orville Wright and Wilbur Wright are already working on such a flying machine."

"So *you* could invent a plane that flies higher."

"No."

"Lower."

"No."

"Faster."

"No."

"Slower."

"No."

"Well, perhaps you could invent a plane that shows movies and gives out little bags of peanuts while people are flying."

"No."

"Well, perhaps you could invent the airport."

"What's an airport, dear sweet mother?"

"I don't know, my son, you're the inventor."

"I think I should leave now," said Thomas.

"Right," said his mother, carefully leaving out the silent 'W' as she put away the pancakes without giving him any.

Eight

A little over a week later, as Bernie was driving him home from his first one-mile walk, Edison blurted out, "I haven't eaten in 11 days!"

"Oh my! Do you want me to stop for pancakes?" Bernie asked. "There's an LHOP* just down the road."

"No! No pancakes! I already spoke too much about pancakes in the last chapter!" said Edison. That totally confused Bernie, who was quite sure that Edison knew that he hadn't been in the last chapter.

"Would you rather I take us to Alexander

*Local House of Pancakes

Graham Taco Bell? Or…"

"No food! I am inventing something amazing, and I cannot do it on a full stomach!"

Bernie looked at Edison and saw a look of determination that told him to stop talking and keep driving.

Which is just what he did. For four hours. During that time, Edison's unfed stomach was growling quite a bit—it even formed words and sentences, at various points saying, "Feed me," "I is hungry," and "Does anyone have change for a quarter?"

Finally, after Bernie had driven around the same block 418 times, Edison finally

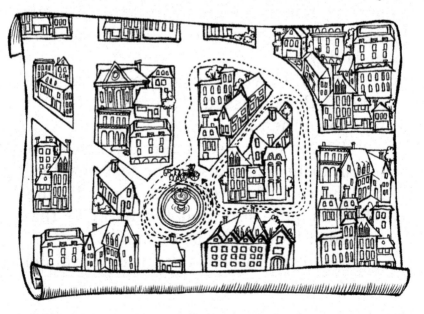

said something (from his mouth, not his stomach).

"Stop the horse and buggy! I think I just invented something better than a flying machine! Better than the self-feeding dog!

Better than the inflatable cream pie! Better than *anything*!"

Bernie pulled on the reins until the horse and buggy came to a screeching stop and said, "What is it?"

"I call it the phonograph!" Edison exclaimed.

"Why the phonograph?" Bernie asked.

"Because it's a phonograph!" Edison told him. "What else would I call it?"

Nine

Of course, phonographs aren't very popular these days, but you've probably seen one or two somewhere, sometime. It's a device that allows you to put a flat black platter on a revolving turntable, place a needle on it, and music plays as it spins.

When Edison got back home, he had a light tuna snack and then invented the phonograph record so that he'd have something to listen to.

Suddenly, Edison (and many, many people not named Edison) could enjoy voice recordings—and beautiful music—anytime.

Thomas Edison's invention of the phonograph and phonograph record led to many future developments in sound recording. Remember that and say, "Thank you, Mr. Edison" every time you listen to music. Because without Thomas Edison, chances are you'd have to hire Lady Gaga whenever you want to hear her songs at home, and that could get quite expensive.

By the way, when Bernie first saw the phonograph, he thought it was a device for spinning pancakes to make them more delicious. Fortunately, Edison grabbed Bernie's hand right before he was about to play a pancake on the phonograph.

That would have been a disaster—and probably not at all pleasant to listen to.

Which brings to mind a good lesson to learn from Bernie and Thomas: *never, never, never* put food of any kind on a phonograph, or stereo, or entertainment system. Today's advanced technology does not create music from food items—though many of the top hits played on Radio Disney often sound like egg salad, pickled beets, and coleslaw being funneled through a paper shredder.

And don't do that either.

Ten

Have you ever watched a cartoon and seen a character have a really good idea—and a light bulb pops up above his or her head? A light bulb is often used to indicate that the person has had a fantastic thought.

Well, while everyone knows (and you're about to find out) that Edison invented the light bulb, only six people in America and one person in New Zealand are aware that when Edison thought of the light bulb for the first time, a bunch of carrots popped up over his head.

Edison had been working in his lab for over 20 minutes a day for almost a whole weekend…and he was about to stop because of darkness when he said to himself, "If only I could work later by making some indoor sunlight."

He then said, "Why am I talking to myself? I don't know. Stop it. Who said that? I did. Are you talking to me? No, you're talking to you. Thomas? Yes, it's me, Thomas. How have you been? I've been fine, and how am I?"

The conversation went on and on, until Thomas had run out of interesting things to say to himself.

Then he had a terrific idea—he'd invent the light bulb! That's when the carrots

appeared, though he didn't see them right away, because it was dark. But when he reached up to scratch his head—as many inventors do when trying to think of something—he felt the carrots and knew he was onto something special.

Thomas waited until the sun came up the next morning (he spent the long hours slowly eating carrots in the dark and thinking of things to talk to himself about). And when it was light, he quickly toiled and tinkered and tinkered and toiled until...he had developed the light bulb!

And he knew that was a good idea later that day, when he invented the lamp—and a light bulb popped up above his head.

Hard to believe? Perhaps. But no harder to believe than the story of any truly great invention. The wheel? Wow. The pretzel? Perfection. The shoe? Sensational. The comb? Cool. And so on.

Eleven

By all accounts, Thomas Edison was a man who believed that a good idea could come from anywhere. Anywhere.

Once, when his barber was giving him a haircut and said, "Everyone voted, and they elected mother"...

...Edison heard the final three words as "the electric motor" and invented it.

Another time, when his barber was giving him a haircut and said, "Mother lost the election this time, and she's very sad. I wish I could take her to the movies"...

...Edison realized that there were no such things as movies and he invented the motion picture camera. Remember that and say, "Why, oh why did you do that, Mr. Edison?" every time you see a rotten movie.

And while Thomas Edison didn't invent the car, once it was invented, Edison put himself to work on creating a really, really, really good battery for it.

It took over six years, thousands of electrical parts, and nearly 100 pounds of chocolate pudding...but finally, Edison was able to step back and behold the finished battery (the chocolate pudding wasn't part of the invention; he just liked eating it).

Twelve

Thirteen is often considered an unlucky number, and this is the chapter right before chapter thirteen, so this seems like the right time to explain how Thomas Edison was quite an unlucky man.

For example, he and Bernie played "I'm Thinking of a Number Between 1 and 25" well over 5,000 times. And Edison never once guessed the number that Bernie had in mind.

See, Bernie *always* thought of 19 as his number, and Edison missed it the first time (he'd guessed 5), and then each time they played after that, Edison developed complex

math formulations in his mind and assumed Bernie would switch to a different number. But Bernie never did.

And when it came time for Edison to think of a number, he too *always* thought of 19, and Bernie never once guessed it. Of course, the difference was that Edison was simply being too mathematical, and Bernie was simply not that smart (he kept forgetting that Edison always thought of 19).

The men played that game for years, until Edison had a brainstorm and they switched to, "I'm Thinking of a Letter

Between C and F"—and both of them kept thinking of D and guessing E.

Edison was also unlucky in that he once stumbled upon a brilliant invention—the television set. Don't get the wrong idea; Edison didn't *invent* the television set, he actually stumbled upon it on the sidewalk. He tripped and fell and broke his hand, and yelled, "Hey, who left that box with the glass front and the little dials on it on the sidewalk right where I was walking?"

A man's voice from a nearby house said, "Sorry, that was me. I invented the television set but I just threw it out."

"Well why did you throw it out?" Edison demanded to know.

"There's nothing good on," answered the voice.

With his unlucky broken hand in a cast for months, Edison single-handedly invented a whole bunch of stuff that changed the lives of men and women on land, sea, and air. It's quite an impressive list of electrical and mechanical breakthroughs, and you'd certainly enjoy reading all about them, but this chapter is, unluckily for you, over.

You kind of feel like Edison now, don't you?

Thirteen

A few chapters ago, you learned of Edison's contributions to the world of motion pictures. To be sure, without his brilliance, the world would never know the joys of sitting in the dark watching images of cars bashing into each other. And to be sure, no one would know the glee of spending $72.50 for 8¢ worth of popcorn drizzled with sticky yellow fake-butter stuff and a bucketful of sugary cola.

But as you take time to admire the man who was Thomas Edison, also pause to reflect on the fact that he wasn't just inventing motion pictures—he was inventing them in 3D. Yes, over 100 years ago, Mr. Edison was working in 3D. For real. 3D.

See, his original lab was in apartment number 2C...but because he wanted to expand and invent larger items, he switched apartments with Beethoven (the owl trainer, not the composer). Beethoven moved into apartment 2C, and Edison switched to the roomier 3D.

Yes indeed, Edison was the first (and only) man to develop motion pictures in 3D. Keep that in mind next time you go to the movies—which are sure to be a lot more entertaining than what Edison could have created in 2C.

Please remember to tell all of your friends about this—but don't do it during the movie, or people will yell, "shhhh"—a word that was, by the way, invented by Edison.

Fourteen

Be it a man or a woman, a baby or a great-grandparent, an inventor's job is to identify a need and take items that have already been thought of and use them in an exciting new way.

As Edison did with the light bulb and all the other inventions you've been so delighted to read about.

In all, Edison was responsible for a whole big messy filing cabinet full of patents. And beyond those hundreds and hundreds and hundreds were countless other inventions that he worked on but didn't have time to perfect or have patented.

Inventions such as the Giraffe-O-Kite. The Knee Polisher. The Gum Wrapper Papper Snapper Glapper. And the Motorized Avocado.

Will future generations see the power and potential of these notions and make them real? Who knows? Perhaps *you* will. Perhaps your friend will. Or your friend's cousin. Or your friend's cousin's piano teacher. Or someone else.

The single thing to keep in mind as a person who now knows *The Lieography of Thomas Edison* is this:

If you're playing "I'm Thinking of a Number Between 1 and 25," it's an excellent idea to guess 19.

Okay, now that you've read *The Lieography of Thomas Edison*, you're probably wondering about the real life story of the great, great inventor.

Well, you're in luck; here are some factual facts about the man. You can believe everything you're about to read, and it'd be great if you check out even more information about him.

Thomas Alva Edison was born in Milan, Ohio on February 11, 1847. He was the youngest of seven children, and they called him Al. The boy wasn't a great student (and, in fact, was home-schooled by his mother), but he showed an early appreciation for chemical experiments and mechanical devices.

At the age of 12, Al set up a printing press and chemistry lab on a train, and started his own newspaper. It was the first one ever printed on a train.

About that time, the young boy lost virtually all of his hearing. Though nearly deaf for the rest of his life, he used that to his advantage; he was able to ignore outside noise and fully concentrate on his work.

A few years later, Edison rescued a toddler from getting injured on a railroad track. To reward his heroism, the little boy's father taught Al railroad telegraphy. Al used that skill in a variety of jobs until 1869, when he decided to devote his time to inventing.

Al received his first patent for an electric voting machine. Soon after, he developed many improvements to existing telegraph technology; he didn't invent Morse Code (Samuel Morse did), but he sure enhanced its functionality.

In 1876, Edison opened a laboratory in Menlo Park, New Jersey. This "invention factory" is where he worked on transmitter technology to improve Alexander Graham Bell's invention of the telephone. He also gave the world the phonograph (the first-ever recording of sound!), as well as the electric light bulb (at that time, people used gas and oil-based lighting), the fuel cell battery, dictation machinery, and the basis for motion picture technology.

Near the end of his life, Edison was working on an alternative to rubber (his friend Henry Ford asked him to come up with something to aid in the manufacture of automobile tires). Edison was getting close— after testing over 17,000 plant species, he developed a way to produce rubber from Goldenrod weed—but sadly, he passed away on October 18, 1931.

In all, Thomas Alva Edison ("The Wizard of Menlo Park") recorded 1,093 United States patents for items that truly affect our daily lives through communication, power, entertainment, and in many other ways.

Wow, was he a man of invention!

Author's Bio

Alan Katz has written more than 40 highly acclaimed children's books, including *Take Me Out of the Bathtub and Other Silly Dilly Songs*, *The Day the Mustache Took Over*, *OOPS!, Don't Say That Word!*, *Really Stupid Stories for Really Smart Kids*, and two *Awesome Achievers* titles. Alan has received many state awards for children's literature, and he frequently speaks at literacy conferences and schools around the country.

Alan is also a six-time Emmy-nominated writer for series including *The Rosie O'Donnell Show*, *Taz-Mania*, *Pinkalicious and Peterrific*, numerous Nickelodeon shows, and more. He hosted a long-running game show on SiriusXM's Kids Place Live channel, and he's also created comic books, trading cards, theme park shows, and hundreds of other special projects for kids and their parents.

Illustrator's Bio

Tracy Hill has been working as an illustrator since 1989, creating humorous and whimsical illustrations for clients in the advertising, editorial, and publishing fields. His true passion has been in illustrating children's books.

THANKS FOR READING
The Lieography of Thomas Edison.

Also pick up other Lieographies:

The Lieography of Babe Ruth

The Lieography of Amelia Earhart